LIBRARY MARKETING

Charleston Briefings: Trending Topics for Information Professionals is a thought-provoking series of brief books concerning innovation in the sphere of libraries, publishing, and technology in scholarly communication. The briefings, growing out of the vital conversations characteristic of the Charleston Conference and *Against the Grain*, will offer valuable insights into the trends shaping our professional lives and the institutions in which we work.

The *Charleston Briefings* are written by authorities who provide an effective, readable overview of their topics—not an academic monograph. The intended audience is busy nonspecialist readers who want to be informed concerning important issues in our industry in an accessible and timely manner.

Matthew Ismail, Editor in Chief

LIBRARY MARKETING

From Passion to Practice

JILL STOVER HEINZE

Published in the United States of America by
ATG LLC (Media)
Manufactured in the United States of America

DOI: http://dx.doi.org/10.3998/mpub.9944237

ISBN 978-1-941269-15-2 (paper)
ISBN 978-1-941269-19-0 (e-book)

against-the-grain.com

CONTENTS

ACKNOWLEDGMENTS

As with all my endeavors, I am humbled and grateful to have had the support of friends, family, and colleagues in writing this brief. The University of Virginia Library has been gracious in allowing me time for this project. Thank you to Chris Ruotolo, Todd Burks, Jeff Hill, Dave Ghamandi, Dave Griles, Annette Stalnaker, and folks on my user experience team for reading drafts and letting me talk through my ideas, challenging them when needed. I am particularly grateful to Melinda Baumann for contributing her keen editorial talents to this work and to my peer reviewer for nudging me to be bold. I appreciate the patience of my husband, Mike, with my late-night and weekend writing sessions. Finally, I am thankful for the Charleston Conference for welcoming my point of view and for Matthew Ismail's unwavering patience.

INTRODUCTION

Most professional discourse among librarians presumes that reconciling marketing practices with our librarian sensibilities is a trivial matter, easily accomplished by launching a connect-the-dots marketing campaign. Alternatively, some assert that marketing is somehow alien or inappropriate for libraries. Even when librarians do address marketing, we focus mainly on the *how* of marketing practices and less on the *what* and *why*. Yet practicalities demand just the opposite—fully understanding the concept of marketing must *precede* sound marketing practice.

Marketing, a bundle of tools and concepts originating in the business world, offers librarians a proven means to advance confidently through uncertainty while allowing us to demonstrate effectively the value we provide to stakeholders. When implemented properly, marketing allows us to create real value for users who would benefit most from our efforts while overcoming marketplace pitfalls that would otherwise derail us. Unfortunately, marketing's potential to secure libraries' success is too often stymied by our preconceptions. Namely, we tend to recognize that marketing can be useful, but we are generally leery of it, if not outright opposed to it. When it comes to librarians, marketing is a tough sell.

What we librarians lack is a deep appreciation of marketing as it relates to our own library service imperatives. Understanding, creating, and accepting a form of marketing that is not only palatable to us but also desirable in libraries is critical to leveraging its impressive potential. It is simply not enough to "go through the motions" of plugging in marketing tactics ad hoc. Librarians need to internalize marketing's true meaning and implications so that we can lead with it rather than be at the mercy of some generic marketing checklist that does not accommodate our values. Consequently, this is not a how-to book. I will not employ the outward-in approach of mindlessly following the marketing dictates that anyone can discover doing a quick Google search. Instead, I will look at marketing from inside of librarianship. I will weigh marketing's merits in order to do the important work of selling marketing to my audience before attempting to apply it beyond.

STARTING WHERE WE ARE
The Uneasy Library-Marketing Relationship

In fairness to librarians, marketing is an ongoing challenge for all organizations in that nearly everyone is trying to figure out innovative ways to connect with customers who are increasingly savvy and saturated with information. But in libraries, the challenge is compounded by the historical baggage librarians attach to marketing itself. The problem with introducing marketing into libraries is not that there is a dearth of tools, talent, thought leaders, education, or activity. Anemic budgets can be a limiting factor, but a lot of beneficial marketing can be done inexpensively. The more entrenched source of library marketing malfunction is deeply rooted in our professional identity and, subsequently, difficult to resolve. Namely, librarians distrust marketing. Of course, there are exceptions, but for many of us, putting on our business hats feels like wearing an ill-fitting garment—it is uncomfortable, awkward, and off-putting.

To be sure, marketing and libraries are not natural allies; some would argue that they are antagonists. While marketing draws from other disciplines like psychology and education, at its core, it is chiefly and traditionally a business activity—a means of getting products to customers while making profits for the companies that create them. Librarianship, at least philosophically, is nearly the mirror opposite. Libraries are generally publicly and/or university-supported institutions that exist to provide a societal good. The "profits" we seek are an informed, empowered citizenry. We are dedicated to making information as widely and freely available as possible. Circulation, but not of currency, fuels the library ethos. Overlaying business imperatives onto libraries can feel like a betrayal of our core values, our users, and our place in society.

Even with this endemic trepidation, marketing activities are commonplace in libraries and library organizations. More than a third of recent library job postings required some sort of marketing duties (McClelland, 2014, p. 362), and marketing competencies are part of many library science curriculums. Our myriad professional associations have also embraced marketing in the form of awards and recognitions, interest groups, committees, dedicated conferences and conference tracks, and shared marketing resources like planning templates, collateral, tool kits, tips, best practices, and consultant directories. In addition, this investment in marketing thought and materials has been fruitful for some libraries. One noteworthy example is the Association of College and Research Libraries' (ACRL) 2017 Excellence in Academic Libraries Award winner, Santa Clara University Library. The library was recognized for its successful assessment of user needs resulting in service development including "a personal librarian service, a robust information literacy program (incorporating Special Collections), and faculty workshops series on integrating research into assignments" (American Library Association, 2017), all of which resulted from applying a marketing-savvy perspective.

Despite all of the marketing activities librarians have increasingly taken on, it seems that collectively we are still searching for the perfect marketing recipe. Even in our successes, we are still left wanting in recognition and visibility. In the series of ACRL-commissioned essays *New Roles for the Road Ahead*, contributor Steven Bell (2015) related an incident about the Middle States Commission on Higher Education's (MSCHE) efforts to revamp its college and university education standards in 2014. Surprisingly, the body that once championed information literacy standards nearly eliminated them solely because its members assumed information literacy was so intrinsic that it no longer merited special attention. Bell elaborated on this irony, speculating,

> As higher education experiences radical change, in what other ways will academic librarians demonstrate the curse of being too successful for their own good? Faculty and students are so accustomed to the highly efficient delivery of digital scholarly content to their desktops and devices that they no longer

are more insulated from market pressures than their public librarian counter-parts, as well as those in reference and technical services had the least positive views of marketing. Rumblings of antipathy made their way into comments, with some arguing that applying business-style marketing does not work in libraries. One complained that "glitzy marketing has no place in a serious intel-lectual setting" (Parker, Kaufman-Scarborough, & Parker, 2007, p. 331), while another respondent who appreciated marketing nevertheless felt it siphoned resources from "essential activities of collection development" (p. 334).

With such ambivalence toward marketing inherent in the library profes-sion even among librarians who do marketing well, is it any surprise that marketing is not as successful as it could be in libraries? When substantive marketing fails to flourish, there is evidence that we should pay attention to the disparity between our outward-facing marketing actions and our internal structures and cultural predispositions. When we do not enjoy doing some-thing or believe in it beyond a superficial level, it is unlikely that we will per-severe in doing it or do as good a job as possible. It is even more unlikely that we will promulgate that activity effectively within our organizations. Instead, the result is halfhearted and reactive; such intermittent efforts do not contain the requisite sustained support to achieve demonstrable outcomes.

MOVING FORWARD
Marketing Fundamentals

The short definition of marketing is that it is a means of creating value for people. I do not know any librarians who would feel in any way at odds with this purpose, even if they dispute the merits of specific tactics. A core requirement for a more functional relationship with marketing is an understanding of what it is, what it is not, and its basic tenets and methods. Once librarians know what modern marketing is beyond unfortunate stereotypes and gut reactions, they are likely to find that it is not as alienating as it might first seem.

As far as formalized, well-established marketing definitions go, the American Marketing Association (AMA, 2013) espouses an expansive one: "Marketing is the activity, set of institutions, and processes for creating, communicating, delivering, and exchanging offerings that have value for customers, clients, partners, and society at large" (para. 2). It is worth noting that based on the AMA's definition, marketing is not just an activity. It encompasses institutions and processes, which illuminates how central marketing is within organizations. Adhering to the full spirit of this definition, marketing is relevant to just about anything anyone working in a library does—buying the right books and online resources, arranging them attractively on shelves, making them discoverable online, providing friendly expertise, creating informational resource guides, curating and maintaining spaces for utilizing materials, and so forth. Marketing's centrality and pervasiveness are among its most important qualities that librarians need to recognize, adopt, and evangelize.

Building on this definition to weigh tactical considerations, we learn that, in addition to being broadly applicable, marketing is innately compatible with our operations and service philosophies. Without getting bogged down with marketing minutia, the four high-level categories of marketing activities are

1. designing and developing products and services to meet people's needs;
2. determining the right level of effort, time, or money customers should spend to obtain the products or services;
3. figuring out how to get the products and services to the people who need them; and
4. telling people about the products and services.

Marketing texts sum up these tasks as "The Four *Ps*": (1) product, (2) price, (3) place, and (4) promotion (Kahn, 2014, p. 95). Despite all of the work that goes into each of these important areas, most people, even many marketers, identify marketing exclusively with number 4 (promotion). Promotion includes marketing's most easily observed output, including advertisements, fundraising events, social media campaigns, and so on. Unfortunately, promotion's close association with marketing gives the rest of marketing short shrift. As far as librarians are concerned, equating marketing with promotion is like judging a book by its cover. And more detrimental, if librarians focus on promotion at the expense of the other activities, then they neglect the most important aspect of marketing—creating value for users.

To understand better this tendency to equate promotion and marketing, try for a moment to think about a service you would like to introduce in your library or a languishing one you would like to improve. Now imagine that you are forbidden to promote that service. You cannot hang a flyer, post a photo to Instagram, or even send an e-mail. How would you go about marketing it? Which aspects of the service would you focus on changing or creating? You might ask yourself important, necessary questions about the service, such as what problems it addresses; who it is intended for and what you know about them; whether someone else is already doing something similar and how what you offer is better; what patrons expect; how, when, and where the service is used; and so on. These kinds of questions about the broader marketplace—including competitors, user behavior, use cases, and market demographics and needs—are exactly the sorts of questions marketers need to ask to make sure offerings are relevant, needed, accessible, and perhaps even sought-after. By avoiding reliance on pushing communications out to people in hopes of persuading them to want our service, we free ourselves to think deeply about how we might adapt our services in order to create something our users want to begin with. Making this intentional distinction is fundamental for any attempt to adopt marketing.

COMING TO TERMS
You Get the Marketing You Make

Marketing's close association with damaging or trivial business outcomes has generated a goodwill deficit with many consumers. The deficit is even more acute among librarians due to the uneasy relationship between marketing and libraries.

What is important for librarians to keep in mind is that marketing is only as good or bad as one makes it. Unethical practices and private-sector intrusions into public domains are legitimately concerning, but adopting marketing practices does not absolve wrongdoings or make us complicit with them. A more productive way to view marketing is as a *means*, not an end. Embracing marketing grants us the ability to wield all of the tools at our disposal to give our mission the best chance of success, and it does not require resigning ourselves to unethical practices or inauthentic representations of who we are and what we offer. The choice is one we have to make mindfully: We can choose to be dismissive of marketing and subsequently forgo all the knowledge and proven methods we could leverage, or we can wholeheartedly welcome marketing into our organizations to hone it for our own needs.

One could argue that marketing has existed in some form or another for as long as people have exchanged goods. Though marketing principles, theories, frameworks, and practices have formalized and evolved over time, exchanging goods for items of value—the essence of marketing—is something of a human constant. During that long history, marketing's presence in robust economies has become ubiquitous.

While marketing may be ever-present, its reputation seems to be mixed at best and abysmal at worst—and not without good reason. Take, for example, the egregiously unethical and socially devastating advertising sponsored by the lead industry in the mid-20th century, whereby industry leaders rebuffed any attempt to restrict its product despite known public health risks. For decades after the 1920s, the lead industry churned out ads promoting the hazardous substance even to families and children, going so far as to distribute coloring books containing instructions on how to prepare lead paint (Rosner & Markowitz, 2013)!

What could generously be called misleading and annoying advertising persists today, prompting legislators to rein in ads for products like tobacco and regulate e-mail communications.[1] Even the promotion of seemingly innocuous luxury and convenience products is cited by marketing detractors as wasteful attempts to part people from their money by enticing them to buy knickknacks and status symbols they do not truly need, cluttering homes, roadways, and landfills.

We must remarket marketing within the library profession so that we feel more invested in and comfortable with it. To do so, it is helpful to recognize the ways in which modern marketing is increasingly aligned with our professional values and goals. Therefore, we need to move beyond the American Marketing Association's useful but basic marketing definition to a more nuanced view that will resonate with librarians.

Marketing luminary Philip Kotler has authored dozens of seminal texts on marketing and is the S. C. Johnson & Son Professor of International Marketing at the Kellogg School of Management at Northwestern University. Among his many publications, Kotler coauthored the 2010 book *Marketing 3.0* (Kotler, Kartajaya, & Setiawan, 2010), in which the authors argue that marketing has evolved from a product- and organization-oriented activity—which they call Marketing 1.0—to a more customer-centric and socially conscious one. Their analysis is particularly helpful for librarians who are unaware of marketing's dynamism and increasing harmony with our own goals.

---

1. See, for example, the Federal Trade Commission's compliance guide to the CAN-SPAM Act at https://www.ftc.gov/tips-advice/business-center/guidance/can-spam-act-compliance-guide -business.

In their book, Kotler et al. (2010) trace marketing's progress through three stages—Marketing 1.0, 2.0, and 3.0—as follows:

- Marketing 1.0 can be understood by imagining a factory: A factory churns out a bunch of widgets, and the marketers (salespeople, advertisers, distributors, etc.) are enlisted to push those widgets out into customers' hands for a profit. Marketing 1.0 is a main culprit in establishing marketing's questionable reputation, since it is more focused on unloading stock than on meeting customer needs.
- Kotler et al. argue that the next phase in marketing's evolution is Marketing 2.0, a shift from the widget factory mind-set to one that puts serving the needs and desires of customers at the forefront (like the AMA's definition).
- From Marketing 2.0, marketing has moved on to yet another stage, Marketing 3.0. As Kotler et al. describe it, "Companies practicing Marketing 3.0 have bigger missions, visions, and values to contribute to the world; they aim to provide solutions to address problems in the society. Marketing 3.0 lifts the concept of marketing to the arena of human aspirations, values, and spirit" (Kotler, Kartajaya, & Setiawan, 2010, p. 4). They argue that Marketing 3.0 firms feel compelled by the impact of massive social and cultural forces such as globalization, environmental degradation, and spiritual uncertainties to create offerings that address the whole "human spirit."

In supporting their argument, Kotler et al. cite a number of companies that behave in ways consonant with Marketing 3.0 principles. Timberland, for instance, is an environmentally aware footwear and apparel producer that closely adheres to a green business model. The company fulfills its green goals through rigorous self-imposed environmental standards for producing its entire line of products so that they remain faithful to their social mission. As the company states, "At Timberland, we hold ourselves accountable for what goes into our products as well as how they're made, and we're constantly seeking innovative solutions to reduce their environmental impact" (Timberland, n.d., para. 5).

While a Marketing 3.0 strategy like Timberland's represents an evolution in its corporate mind-set and accountabilities, libraries were Marketing 3.0

organizations from "birth." Consider the American Library Association's equally aspirational and slightly business-oriented expression of libraries' societal contributions as outlined in its current "Libraries Transform" promotion campaign: "Libraries transform lives. Libraries transform communities. Librarians are passionate advocates for lifelong learning. Libraries are a smart investment" (American Library Association, n.d., para. 8). Given libraries' distinguished record of public and community service, today's corporate marketing philosophy is catching up to resemble the views librarians have held for decades. Marketing and librarianship are becoming intellectually closer, at least as embodied by Kotler et al.'s articulation and the work of other forward-thinking marketers. As a result, we can fruitfully look to Marketing 3.0–like behaviors to help us imagine concrete, compatible ways of applying our own ideals throughout our libraries. Moreover, we can feel good about doing so.

Looking at business examples is helpful in the case of libraries because even though librarians tend to be aligned intellectually and emotionally with the drive to address large-scale societal needs and nurture people's aspirations, holistic library implementations of comprehensive marketing approaches are scarce. In order to achieve the kind of insight into personal and social needs necessary to coalesce a sound user-focused strategy, organizations need to focus their activities on the people they serve. This means insinuating robust user feedback mechanisms into our operations so that we may regularly solicit, receive, analyze, and distribute that feedback and apply the insights gained effectively and purposefully to service designs and improvements. In fact, in a "true" modern marketing organization, *all* functions of the business work together on *all* aspects of service (or product) development to identify and address the needs and wants of its customers—an idea generally referred to as the "marketing concept" (Perreault & McCarthy, 2005, p. 17).

Rarely, though, do librarians extend this concept as fully into their operations as Northern Kentucky University's Steely Library did. Steely Library is an example of a library that has established the requisite conditions for Marketing 3.0–type success on an organizational scale. Steely librarians took on this challenge of changing what its leadership identified as old-fashioned thinking about marketing to a model that is more responsive to the people it serves (Almquist, 2014). Specifically, library leadership created two permanent work teams: a marketing work team (MWT) and an assessment work team (AWT). MWT staff conduct market research and handle external and internal communications, while AWT staff obtain internal operational and survey data from functional units. Librarians positioned the teams centrally within the organization to work closely together and with the library's service units to direct the library's energies toward acting upon demonstrable user desires and generating an ongoing cycle of feedback and responsiveness.

While this approach does not guarantee success, what sets Steely Library apart is that its librarians imposed a formal structural and cultural commitment to marketing and user accountability. By making responsiveness to users intrinsic to their operations, Steely librarians are well positioned to bring the full force of their efforts to bear on identifying and resolving user needs.

STEERING WITH YOUR COMPASS

Market With Your Mission and Your Users

As in the Steely Library example, we need to step back from the tactical marketing considerations—such as how we get the word out about something—in order to tend to strategic considerations first. With limited time and resources, every marketing-related action we take should result in an intentional impact to deliver offerings with meaning and value to people. In fact, it is the cumulative effect of everyday actions across all of our touchpoints—not the big, splashy, one-off promotions—that adds up to make the most significant marketing impacts in users' minds. Therefore, there is a risk to piloting too many scattershot communications to see if a few people respond (in the style of Marketing 1.0 thinking). In worst-case scenarios, that kind of hodgepodge marketing damages libraries' reputations among users, as it presents a disjointed, incoherent view of who they are. Instead, we need to do some hard work building our missions—the bedrock of our offerings—with help from our users in order to devise the mission-related imperatives that we carry in all interactions and communications with users.

Too many "marketing" planning meetings lead to dead ends or indeterminate results because there is no agreement on who we should focus our efforts on, the purpose of those efforts, and how we would determine success. Teams I have worked on are good at identifying large groups that we want to inform ("We want students to know about our online chat service!") but not so good at honing in on important details like specific user groups to target, why those groups should care about a service, how a service fits into their lives, and importantly, articulating how these actions support a greater mission. And many teams forget to discuss whether the service is helpful to begin with!

To help understand the importance of mission-driven marketing, consider how it plays out in the corporate world. Starbucks, for example, is generally recognized for its savvy marketing, but it faced serious challenges to its identity during the Great Recession, starting in December 2007. After returning as Starbucks's CEO in early 2008, Howard Schultz complained that the company had expanded the number of stores too broadly at the expense of its key core values—the quality of its coffee and in-store experience. As stores proliferated, coffee quality suffered, service became erratic and impersonal, and a new expansive food menu clouded the company's value proposition (and, much to Schultz's chagrin, created odors that competed with the coffee's aroma). While these strategies yielded near-term profits that satisfied shareholders for a while, they also weakened the sense of mission and values that would sustain the company long-term. And in fact, there was pressure on stock prices as the accumulation of corners cut cascaded down to the front lines. As Schultz realized, tactics need to be reconciled with ethos; otherwise, Starbucks would risk undermining what was truly foundational and important to the organization. As he insightfully summed it up in his autobiographical book *Onward*, "Every brand has inherent nuances that, if compromised, will eat away at its equity regardless of short-term returns" (Schultz & Gordon, 2012, p. 175).

Implicit in Schultz's observation, and important for us to recognize, is that an organization must know what it stands for and stay true to its mission. Though we share high-level common values, every library fills a particular niche informed by the special needs of their stakeholders. Some libraries specialize in the support of cutting-edge cross-disciplinary research, others concentrate on the preservation and digitization of rare materials, while still others focus on providing technical equipment and expertise necessary for specialized research. A primary concern for each library is to discover, along with its users, the "inherent nuances" that set it apart from others in users' minds. We should safeguard and emphasize these nuances in our marketing plans or else we are in danger of fading into an undifferentiated crowd of competitors. Marketing should never entice us to shortchange those nuances; rather, it should give us the means to leverage them.

Like Schultz, successful marketing leaders today credit tending to mission above all as the secret to their accomplishments. A recent *Forbes* article reported on this year's American Marketing Association New York's marketing Hall of Famers—four honorees with experience working for global brands like P&G and IBM, who agree that adhering to sound mission and values is what differentiates marketplace winners from the rest. These distinguished honorees ascribe to a Marketing 3.0–like philosophy in that they recognize the importance of connecting their missions with their customers on an emotional level. As the author notes,

> They share the awareness that, in order to remain relevant—to keep mattering to people—organizations must have a guiding purpose above and beyond what they do or sell; organizations must remain true to their values, hold fast to their DNA; and organizations must be able to tell their stories in a compelling and authentic way through the lens of their purpose. (Adamson, 2017, para. 4)

Far from an esoteric exercise, making a mission work in practice is a fraught but integral aspect of library marketing. We are keenly aware of this challenge in library spheres as we work, and in some cases struggle, to adapt our mission in a context of information abundance and rapid technological advances. One example that has evoked strong opinions about libraries' futures is Arizona State University's (ASU) Hayden Library renovation. In recognition of the declining use of print books and simultaneous increase in electronic resource and space demands, ASU's University Librarian James O'Donnell is looking to the retail sector and Amazon specifically for innovative models of library resource delivery, including the use of drones and novel ways to showcase library materials by exhibiting them on a rotating basis and retaining only a small selection of books on site. O'Donnell argues that an online resource-oriented library "means changing your service model, your staffing structure and organization" (Straumsheim, 2017, para. 7). Dramatic shifts like this force librarians to ask questions like, Which of these choices bolster our mission, and which ones weaken it? Which decisions illuminate our inherent nuances, and which put them and our values at risk? For some, ASU's move represents an unwelcome displacement of library values for industry ones, evidenced by ASU librarians' choice of the term "fulfillment center" to describe its off-site storage facility. Others view the project as a logical necessity in adapting to modern realities and space pressures.

Addressing which strategies to pursue as extensions of a library's inviolable character and deciding which elements should give way to the needs of today and tomorrow is exceptionally difficult. On the one hand, we are obligated to be responsive to the expressed and implied needs of our users, but on the other, we have to guard against sacrificing our values to the whims of frivolous fads or shortsighted pressures.

One way to find the right mix of responsiveness and mission fidelity is by co-stewarding our mission with our users. Here too marketing knowledge can be of help to librarians.

To understand why this librarian-user partnership is important, it is helpful to know some marketing realities when it comes to the nature of services like the ones libraries provide. Services are a type of product, but they are different in important respects from physical products like cars and microchips. Library services are not tangible goods. They cannot be touched, eaten, or packaged. While one can see evidence of a service in the form of brochures, personal interactions, and so on, the service itself is invisible. In addition, marketers point out that services are also inseparable (Coldren, 2006, para. 3), meaning that they are "consumed" at the same moment they are created. Consider, for example, a reference transaction. Librarians do not have a ready supply of answers sitting on shelves to hand out to users. Instead, we conduct reference interviews to ascertain users' needs and tailor our responses to specific requests through conversations and participation with users.

These defining characteristics demonstrate that users themselves are part of the invisible structure of the very services we make. There is simply no way to create a service *for* users. By definition, we can only create services *with* users. And the perceived value and quality of those services exist only in users' minds, well beyond librarians' control. What we can choose, however, is to acknowledge this interrelationship and purposefully make opportunities to increase users' involvement at all stages of our service development to improve the chances that library services will resonate with them. Finding these opportunities is an area ripe for marketing innovation in libraries.

Take as one example patron-driven acquisitions (PDA). PDA is an approach to collection-building where users trigger the purchase of materials on demand, either directly by making a request for the purchase of a print item or automatically by using an electronic item a predetermined number of times. In effect, PDA opens up the once-closed acquisition ecosystem to enable users to have a direct say in what materials libraries buy. Furthermore, this user involvement is in alignment with libraries' mission of matching people with needed information.

Blindly pursuing our mission without regard for those who help us define, clarify, hone, and achieve it opens libraries up to problems of mission ambiguity and, consequently, irrelevance. We see inklings of this danger in some recent analyses. Ithaka S+R's most recent U.S. Library Survey of academic library directors provides some indications of library–stakeholder disconnects that may be the result of not partnering with our end users to calibrate our mission and purpose as well as we could. These results include the following findings:

- Three-quarters of library directors surveyed rated their library's role as a resource archive as important, while just 58% of them thought their supervisors agreed (Wolff, 2017, p. 13).
- Faculty members rated the role of buying needed resources as the library's most important function, while library directors cited their role in supporting undergraduate research as most important (p. 14).
- Only half of directors reported having clear collections strategies that drove decision making, and less than half reported that their library had a clear, broadly accepted vision on campus for the use of its spaces (p. 44).

In light of these gaps, it may not be surprising that of the 13 sources respondents were asked to rank in this survey, library directors ranked the top three influencers of their library's strategic priorities as themselves, librarians/professional staff, and the provost/chief academic officer. Student groups and influential faculty were ranked sixth and eighth, respectively (p. 19).

A white paper by McGraw-Hill Education (2016) unearthed similar evidence of disconnects in its survey of librarians and faculty, concluding, "There is misalignment in what makes libraries most useful, and therefore misalignment in how their success should be measured and how budgets should be allocated" (p. 1). For instance, the study found that a whopping 88% of faculty felt the library's primary purpose was offering "access to information," whereas only 43% of librarians responded the same (p. 3). Despite the overall finding that faculty believe libraries effectively meet their communities' needs, it is concerning that librarians must overcome such a towering marketing hurdle to meaningfully connect with faculty who have very different ideas about the basic function of libraries.

Gaps like these are precisely why focusing on promotion alone falls flat. Without a shared understanding and mental model about what a library is and does, communication with stakeholders is impossible. It is not that one perspective is more valid than the other but that missions need to be tended to collaboratively with users via ongoing dialogue, partnership, and feedback in order to have a shared understanding to base a relationship upon. No amount of "push" communications like posters, e-mails, or newsletters can do this work.

KEEPING IT REAL
Let Your Metrics Be Your Guide

In library marketing, metrics should keep us honest about how well we are achieving our missions within the context of our available resources. Metrics are the guideposts needed to tell us when we are being inefficient or ineffective for our stakeholders so we can make immediate corrections and to identify what is working well that we should retain or emphasize. Librarians need to build these warning signals into marketing planning in the form of measurements and feedback that can keep activities finely tuned to produce demonstrable benefits for users.

Disney movie fans may remember the sage advice given to Pinocchio as he set out to make his way in the world: Let your conscience be your guide. In a similar way, metrics are a means of keeping our activities aligned with our mission, which we should in turn align with user needs. When marketing, it is tempting to get caught up in doing stuff like designing T-shirts, convening workshops, providing consultations, setting up event booths, publishing videos, and tweeting photos. Ultimately, while these activities feel productive, they have no significance outside of how they help or hinder users, nurture our mutual relationship, and further our mission. We need other measurements to help us know if we are hitting the mark.

Librarians deeply feel the importance of this assessment imperative in a general sense. Consider the Association of College and Research Libraries' *2015 Environmental Scan* of the academic landscape, which states, "With higher education under increased scrutiny to demonstrate the value of a post-secondary degree, it is incumbent upon academic libraries and librarians to document and communicate the Library's value in supporting the core mission of the institution" (ACRL Research Planning and Review Committee, 2015, p. 23). It is the value to stakeholders, not the quantity and quality of activities, that counts.

In libraries, just like in marketing, assessment is important but not always straightforward. There is a well-known saying in the advertising world that summarizes this conundrum: "Half my advertising is wasted, I just don't know which half" (Wanamaker, 1999, para. 1). In business, marketers rely on measurements that are financial in nature, but they too need to demonstrate that their work bolsters the organization's core objectives and financial goals, as well as healthy relationships with customers.

Librarians are no strangers to assessment, and discourse in this area is increasingly robust.[2] But when we think about how to assess our marketing effectiveness in particular, we would do well to consider business approaches that could inspire novel ways for us to evaluate our work. Translating metrics from businesses to libraries requires a bit of effort, given that we do not have dollar figures to benchmark against. Compared to librarians, marketers do a better job of thinking about the totality of the service relationship—from the customer and organization perspectives—to determine if the benefits achieved are worth the expenditures of time, money, and effort from all parties. As lean organizations, libraries should pay particular attention to the cost-benefit of its marketing by monitoring the degree of benefit users receive relative to the cost of serving those users.

One example of librarians doing just that is an evaluation conducted by librarians at the College of New Jersey (TCNJ) as they deftly determined whether they should invest in creating and maintaining library-specific social media channels. To do so, they questioned the merits of setting up these channels despite their prevalence among library peers. In textbook marketing fashion, librarians evaluated their college's mission statement, other campus social media efforts, their staffing capacity, and library goals and then surveyed undergraduate students about their social media use. As a result, they

---

2. For an overview of recent thinking in library assessment, see the work presented at the Library Assessment Conference at http://libraryassessment.org/.

declined to establish these channels, opting instead to contribute to existing ones. According to their report,

> While the Library strives to keep up with ever changing technology, decisions need to be made that best meet the needs of the majority of the TCNJ community. For now, developing library-specific social media channels has been put aside so the Library's efforts can stay focused on moving forward in other directions. Projects that are more highly demanded on campus, such as the Library's institutional repository and digital archive need to take priority. (Cowell, 2017, para. 27)

In essence, TCNJ librarians estimated their expected return on investment (ROI) and concluded that this initiative was not a sufficiently impactful use of scarce resources.

The two primary measures necessary to make these calculations are benefits and costs for both the library and the user. Users, not librarians, determine what those benefits are. Assessments, therefore, need to probe into users' perceptions. They should identify what users want to accomplish in terms of concrete goals (e.g., writing a paper, obtaining a grant) and emotional goals (e.g., reduced stress, connecting with peers). We can glean these insights by doing needs assessments and surveys and reviewing transactional data. As part of our investigation, we should inquire about the costs users must "pay" to achieve these benefits and whether those costs are merited. Those costs could take the form of stress level, time, feelings of uncertainty, and so on. Our measures should question user satisfaction and whether the services received seem appropriate for the price tag.

Libraries too should recognize that they have goals and costs and that not all well-intentioned initiatives are profitable enough to pursue, as was the case for TCNJ librarians. In addition, this kind of analysis could help us lower our costs by prompting us to find ways to extend our services to more users with similar needs. To do so, librarians should once again consider their missions and strategic imperatives and translate those imperatives to the measures being collected. If a librarian is seeking to expand the use of scholarly materials and devoting marketing energy toward that end, he or she needs some data points that would, at minimum, help triangulate whether those actions are positively or negatively affecting that outcome. Such measures range from usage statistics to user surveys and personal interviews. Likewise, if a library is promoting scholarly resources on its website, librarians should embed tracking tools to ascertain click-through rates and downloads.

Librarians may think of costs in ways similar to how marketers view them. Marketers, for example, consider the cost of acquiring new customers versus serving existing ones better. Since acquiring new customers is more expensive, think about how to balance your efforts to reach nonusers with more fully serving your regular users. Marketers also size their market to determine how many people they can reasonably expect to reach. If, as in this extreme example, a librarian wants to create an instructional program for all senior, first-generation, female student-athletes who are also science majors, the ROI could be quite low, so he or she should consider expanding the group to help others who share common underlying needs.

MAXIMIZING IMPACT
Be Selective to Be Effective

Market segmentation is the practice of grouping people who share certain characteristics that influence how receptive they are likely to be to your service offerings. As I began to explore in my discussion of metrics and return on investment, marketing is predicated upon the ability to assess a large market of existing and potential customers and divide them into logical subgroups of manageable size. This marketing practice is often hard for librarians to reconcile with their innate desire to serve as many people as possible at all times, but the idea suggests that they can actually serve more people better by not serving everyone equally. While we may not always recognize it, librarians actually practice segmentation all the time. In academic libraries, we commonly think of users in terms of status (undergraduate, graduate, faculty, staff) and affiliation (school, department, community member, home institution). We may even subdivide these groups further, breaking undergraduates down into ranks (freshman, sophomore, junior, and senior). In public libraries, we tailor services to parents, children, seniors, entrepreneurs, and new community arrivals, and we establish branch locations based on population. Consequently, the segmentation concept is not foreign to libraries. More alien to us is the idea that there would be people we do not proactively serve continuously. Each of us wants to serve everyone, but realistically we know we will never see 100% of our potential users. We may welcome any undergraduate into our library, but we know that students whose coursework requires using library materials are much more likely to use library collections. Given these facts, our work could be much more effective if we were to intentionally subdivide and serve this group according to its particular needs. Setting our sights specifically on undergraduates with library assignments puts our focus on studying and solving the most pressing needs of that group, which in turn should make our marketing more relevant and resonant than something aimed at undergraduates generically.

For some, segmentation is a subtle shift in mind-set, while for others it is a major departure from how we think of our users and service imperatives. When we interact with those whom we have identified as our most likely customers and then apply measurements to evaluate the success of those interactions, we are applying our scarce time and resources where they are mostly likely to produce lasting benefits for both our users and our libraries. Indeed, studies show that customers who are satisfied, are committed to keeping a relationship with a brand, and trust an organization are more likely to share positive word of mouth with others (Lang & Hyde, 2013, p. 11), who are then more likely to use the offerings. While it may initially seem counterintuitive, serving a select group well allows a library the goodwill, referrals, and perhaps even increased funds necessary to expand its reach further into that segment and other segments that might have been outside its reach previously.

Another way to use the market segmentation exercise to expand a library's impact is by thinking creatively about how it can extend its current services to expensive-to-acquire new or underserved groups. As a library carves its market, librarians should think about group characteristics and needs that might cause people to react positively to their services. For example, we can consider the many people who walk into libraries in search of space and equipment that will help them to be productive. Surely there is a "Needs to Get Work Done" user segment in almost every library that would be looking for similar things—quiet places, whiteboards, printers, and so on. That segment would likely have people in it who cut across more traditional segments like faculty and students, entrepreneurs, and job seekers. Could a librarian create an innovative service focused on satisfying this particular group? Such creative thinking about segments could help librarians expend resources efficiently while also distinguishing them in the marketplace, giving their libraries heightened visibility.

When it comes to segmentation, therefore, we should not settle for the answer "everyone" when asking, "Who is this service for?" "Who?" is among the most important questions librarians have to answer in their marketing journeys, as it will inform nearly every other decision and should be given the dedicated thought it deserves.

GAINING AN EDGE
Competing for Customers Is Living Your Mission

Entering a competitive state of mind can be a stretch for librarians, but like other marketing-related concepts, the notion of competition carries with it some inaccurate associations. For one, competing does not mean succeeding at the expense of someone else. Organizations can win simultaneously by succeeding in their areas of strength and by cooperating. One only needs to look to the incredible variety of organizations within sectors like retail, higher education, nonprofit, and entertainment to see that many entities can coexist in the same sphere. Think too about library consortia in which librarians build cooperative collections and participate in joint initiatives that would be impossible to take on alone. Moreover, competition affects every organization, no matter how far removed from "business." Librarians face external competition from search engines, bookstores, coffee houses, and entertainment venues, as well as from internal threats such as other units on campus demanding a larger share of the budget. While some of these competitors are very distinct from libraries, our users' experiences with competing organizations influence what they expect we should be able to do for them. (How many times have users said that they expect library catalogs to work like Google or Amazon?) Ignoring competitors is, in effect, ignoring our users' point of view, which is antithetical to both marketing and librarianship.

Peter C. Brinckerhoff (2010), author and marketing consultant for nonprofit organizations, expressed the value of competition in his book

Mission-Based Marketing. In it, he draws from his extensive nonprofit marketing experience to offer readers the following mantra: "Repeat after me: *Competing is not bad. Competing is not immoral.* Competing means continuing to be there to do good works. Competing makes us better. Competing means doing more mission" (p. 25). When we compete, we effectively tell our users that we value their viewpoints and that we have confidence that what we offer is worth their time relative to anything else they could be doing.

You have surely heard the phrase "healthy competition" at some time or another. There is a reason those words are frequently paired—recognizing the strengths of competitors prompts one to stay sharp and current with what is happening in the marketplace. More importantly, competitive pressures nudge organizations to think carefully about the unique value they can deliver to their users. Putting competitive thinking into practice will force you to examine your work in its proper real-world context.

CONCLUSION
Start With the Hard Part

Whenever we give short shrift to difficult conversations about our goals, services, and organizational structures in favor of quick wins and one-off promotions, we have skipped over doing the hard work of real marketing and furthering the cultural acceptance of it. Marketing entails reengaging with our shared purposes and passions as librarians while fully grounding them in our practice with the central idea that marketing orients all of our efforts toward making value for the people who matter most—our users.

Librarians do phenomenal work, and we all want to remain essential, trusted partners in our communities. When we confront severe budget cuts or deep frustration and anxiety about why so many users seem oblivious to what we do and why it is important, applying marketing in its fullest sense is imperative. Merely learning about marketing and how to apply its bevy of tactics is not the answer to securing relevance, and so we need to resist the deceptively convenient idea that if we just could find the right mix of the Four *P*s, execute them, and repeat—*poof!*—we would be overwhelmed by floods of users. As I hope we all recognize by now, marketing well is not that simple, and it certainly is not easy.

This briefing offers more than a tool kit to hammer away at the barriers we contend with—and will always have to contend with—as librarians. Rather, it presents concepts and preconditions for marketing success that are less immediately satisfying than ticking off a series of tasks yet are more likely to sustain our institutions in the long term. Namely, these preconditions include the following:

- A commitment to tending to our mission with the care it deserves as our most important marketing asset and marketplace differentiator. This commitment entails keeping the mission alive by inviting our users to help us understand how to fulfill it as our environment changes, without straying too far from our purpose. We should not accept findings (like Ithaka S+R's) that expose a lack of clear collections strategies and vision for our spaces. If we lack clarity on issues so close to our mission, how can we expect to engage users about them? Achieving mission clarity is an opportunity to work with our users to discover a mission together.

- Organizational structures with embedded feedback mechanisms that orient all of our efforts toward soliciting, evaluating, and solving our users' needs in partnership with our users and keep us accountable to those ends. (Steely Library's reorganization is one attempt at doing so.)

- Opportunities for dialogue within and among libraries, as well as ongoing training that demystifies marketing and exposes the ways marketing thinking is applicable to all operations and service interactions. Achieving the deeper understanding librarians need to succeed at marketing requires creating opportunities to consider and apply its tenets as we carry out our daily work.

- An acceptance of frequent and constant change that marketing demands. Administrators should provide skill training, emotional support, and rewards for risk taking. Because librarians create services with users, we need to adapt those services based on our users' contributions. We also need to draw in and recognize user input and incorporate it into our service planning continuously, which necessitates ongoing change. We may be wrong in how we apply those findings from time to time, but we will never be wrong in being responsive to users.

- Enthusiasm and mechanisms for collecting evidence about the efficacy of librarians' work. Data should not limit but free us to focus on where we create the most value and help us reflect honestly on our progress toward achieving our mission.

Admittedly, this list of conditions includes a tinge of idealism, but it is entirely achievable. The most successful organizations can and do address these requirements of a marketing commitment. Achieving them is the difficult work of marketing and the part that is most tempting to overlook when we can more readily hang up a sign or invent a clever campaign. The problem is that, while those things are easier, they are not marketing, and they are not going to secure our ability to do more of our mission.

We librarians need to come to a philosophical truce with marketing in order to take proper advantage of its promises, a truce that is both appropriate and necessary for our work. The only path to acceptance and subsequent success is honest, ongoing, and purposeful conversation with colleagues, users, and stakeholders to ensure we apply what is useful about marketing in a way that does not usurp the very mission we need to celebrate and make real.

REFERENCES

ACRL Research Planning and Review Committee. (2015, March). *Environmental scan 2015.* Retrieved from http://www.ala.org/acrl/sites/ala.org.acrl/files/content/publications/whitepapers/EnvironmentalScan15.pdf

Adamson, A. (2017, May 5). How Marketing Hall of Famers from Facebook, P&G and IBM shift ahead before it's too late. *Forbes.* Retrieved from https://www.forbes.com/sites/allenadamson/2017/05/05/how-marketing-hall-of-famers-from-facebook-pg-and-ibm-shift-ahead-before-its-too-late/#22e44fae68b7

Almquist, A. (2014). The innovative academic library: Implementing a marketing orientation to better address user needs and improve communication. *Journal of Library Innovation, 5*(1), 43–54.

American Library Association. (2017, January). *2017 ACRL Excellence in Academic Libraries award winners announced* [Press release]. Retrieved from http://www.ala.org/news/press-releases/2017/01/2017-acrl-excellence-academic-libraries-award-winners-announced

American Library Association. (2016). Introduction. In K. Rosa (Ed.), *State of America's libraries report* (pp. 5–6). Retrieved from http://www.ala.org/news/state-americas-libraries-report-2016/introduction

American Library Association. (n.d.). Libraries transform campaign. *Libraries Transform.* Retrieved from http://www.ala.org/transforminglibraries/libraries-transform-campaign

American Marketing Association. (2013). *About AMA.* Retrieved from https://www.ama.org/AboutAMA/Pages/Definition-of-Marketing.aspx

Bell, S. (2015). Evolution in higher education matters to libraries. In N. Allen (Ed.), *New roles for the road ahead: Essays commissioned for ACRL's 75th anniversary* (pp. 13–18). Chicago, IL: Association of College and Resource Libraries. Retrieved from http://www.ala.org/acrl/sites/ala.org.acrl/files/content/publications/whitepapers/new_roles_75th.pdf

Brinckerhoff, P. C. (2010). *Mission-based marketing: Positioning your not-for-profit in an increasingly competitive world* (3rd ed.). Hoboken, NJ: John Wiley & Sons.

Coldren, C. (2006, January 31). Four factors that distinguish services marketing. *Marketing-Profs*. Retrieved from http://www.marketingprofs.com/6/coldren2.asp

Cowell, A. (2017, January 8). Social media at the College of New Jersey Library. *In the Library with the Lead Pipe*. Retrieved from http://www.inthelibrarywiththeleadpipe.org/2017/social-media-tcnj/

Eisenhower, C. (2011, February 2). From cost-center to profit-center: Academic libraries and the corporatization of higher ed [Blog post]. Retrieved from https://www.insidehighered.com/blogs/university_of_venus/from_cost_center_to_profit_center_academic_libraries_and_the_corporatization_of_higher_ed

Khan, M. T. (2014). The concept of "marketing mix" and its elements (A conceptual review paper). *International Journal of Information, Business and Management, 6*(2), 95–107.

Kotler, P., Kartajaya, H., & Setiawan, I. (2010). *Marketing 3.0: From products to customers to the human spirit*. Hoboken, NJ: Wiley.

Lang, B., & Hyde, K. F. (2013). Word of mouth: What we know and what we have yet to learn. *Journal of Consumer Satisfaction, Dissatisfaction & Complaining Behavior, 26*, 1–18.

McClelland, T. (2014). What exactly do you do here? Marketing-related jobs in public and academic libraries. *Journal of Library Administration, 54*(5), 347–367. doi:10.1080/01930826.2014.946736

McGraw-Hill Education. (2016). *The changing role of libraries*. Retrieved from https://learn.mheducation.com/rs/303-FKF-702/images/Whitepaper_AccessEducation_RoleofLibraries_10-2016_v4%20%283%29.pdf

Parker, R., Kaufman-Scarborough, C., & Parker, J. (2007). Libraries in transition to a marketing orientation: Are librarians' attitudes a barrier? *International Journal of Nonprofit and Voluntary Sector Marketing, 12*, 320–337. doi:10.1002/nvsm.295

Perreault, W. D., Jr., & McCarthy, E. J. (2005). *Basic marketing: A global-managerial approach* (15th ed.). Homewood, IL: Irwin.

Rosner, D., & Markowitz, G. (2013, April 23). Why it took decades of blaming parents before we banned lead paint. *The Atlantic*. Retrieved from https://www.theatlantic.com/health/archive/2013/04/why-it-took-decades-of-blaming-parents-before-we-banned-lead-paint/275169/

Schultz, H., & Gordon, J. (2012). *Onward: How Starbucks fought for its life without losing its soul*. Emmaus, PA: Rodale. [Kindle version]. Retrieved from Amazon.com.

Straumsheim, C. (2017, March 24). The library has never been more important. *Inside Higher Ed*. Retrieved from https://www.insidehighered.com/news/2017/03/24/arizona-state-u-library-reorganization-plan-moves-ahead

Timberland. (n.d.). *New product standards set pace to achieve our 2020 goals*. Retrieved from https://www.timberland.com/responsibility/stories/new-product-standards-2020-goals.html

Wanamaker, J. (1999, March 29). Advertising age: The advertising century. Retrieved from http://adage.com/article/special-report-the-advertising-century/john-wanamaker/140185/

Wolff, C. (2017, April 3). *Ithaka S+R US library survey 2016*. Retrieved from http://www.sr.ithaka.org/wp-content/uploads/2017/03/SR_Report_Library_Survey_2016_04032017.pdf

ABOUT THE AUTHOR

Jill Stover Heinze is the director of user experience at the University of Virginia Library. Heinze has worked in academic libraries and in the private sector in competitive intelligence and marketing roles. In 2006, she was recognized as a Library Journal Mover & Shaker for her marketing efforts. She holds a bachelor of arts degree in history from the Ohio State University, a master of science in library science from the University of North Carolina at Chapel Hill, and a certificate in marketing from Virginia Commonwealth University. She lives in Charlottesville, Virginia, with her husband and two children.

www.ingramcontent.com/pod-product-compliance
Lightning Source LLC
Chambersburg PA
CBHW081251040426

42452CB00015B/2790